Please Don't Wake the Animals

To Guillaume,
my son-in-law / *mon beau-fils*,
whose pictures awaken sleeping worlds.

—*M. B.*

For my new grandchild,
Alexis Maria Bond.
Wake up and see the world!

—*H. B.*

Special thanks to Howard Choat, School of Marine Biology and Aquaculture,
James Cook University, Australia; Charles T. Collins, California State University at Long Beach;
and D. Ross Robertson, Smithsonian Tropical Research Institute, Panama.

—*M. B.*

Published by
PEACHTREE PUBLISHERS
1700 Chattahoochee Avenue
Atlanta, Georgia 30318-2112
www.peachtree-online.com

Text © 2008 by Mary Batten
Illustrations © 2008 by Higgins Bond

Art direction by Loraine M. Joyner
Composition by Melanie McMahon Ives

Illustrations created in acrylics on cold press illustration board. Title typeset in International
Typeface Corporation's Tempus Sans; text typeset in ITC's Tempus Sans and Stone Sans.

Printed in Singapore
10 9 8 7 6 5 4 3 2 1
First Edition

Library of Congress Cataloging-in-Publication Data

Batten, Mary.
  Please don't wake the animals / written by Mary Batten ; illustrated by Higgins Bond.
    p. cm.
  ISBN 13: 978-1-56145-393-1 / ISBN 10: 1-56145-393-5
  1. Sleep behavior in animals--Juvenile literature. I. Bond, Higgins, ill. II. Title.
  QL755.3.B38 2008
  591.5'19--dc22
                                        2007031904

Please Don't Wake the Animals

A Book about Sleep

written by Mary Batten

illustrated by Higgins Bond

PEACHTREE
ATLANTA

Shhh. Please don't wake the animals in this book. They are sleeping.

All people sleep. So do all other mammals, like gorillas and bears, whales and bats. Birds sleep, too. Even snakes, fish, and insects have a way of sleeping.

All animals sleep, but some need a lot while others can get by with only a little.

Sleep helps restore animals' energy. When animals sleep, they get in a comfortable position and close their eyes. They get very quiet, and their bodies are much less active than when they are awake. Some animals can sleep through a lot of noise, but others wake up at the slightest sound.

Large mammals usually sleep less than small mammals. African elephants sleep only 3 to 4 hours each day. Most cats sleep around 12 hours, or half a day. Newborn human babies need between 16 and 18 hours of sleep, while most adults need around 8 hours. Some bats sleep almost 20 hours a day.

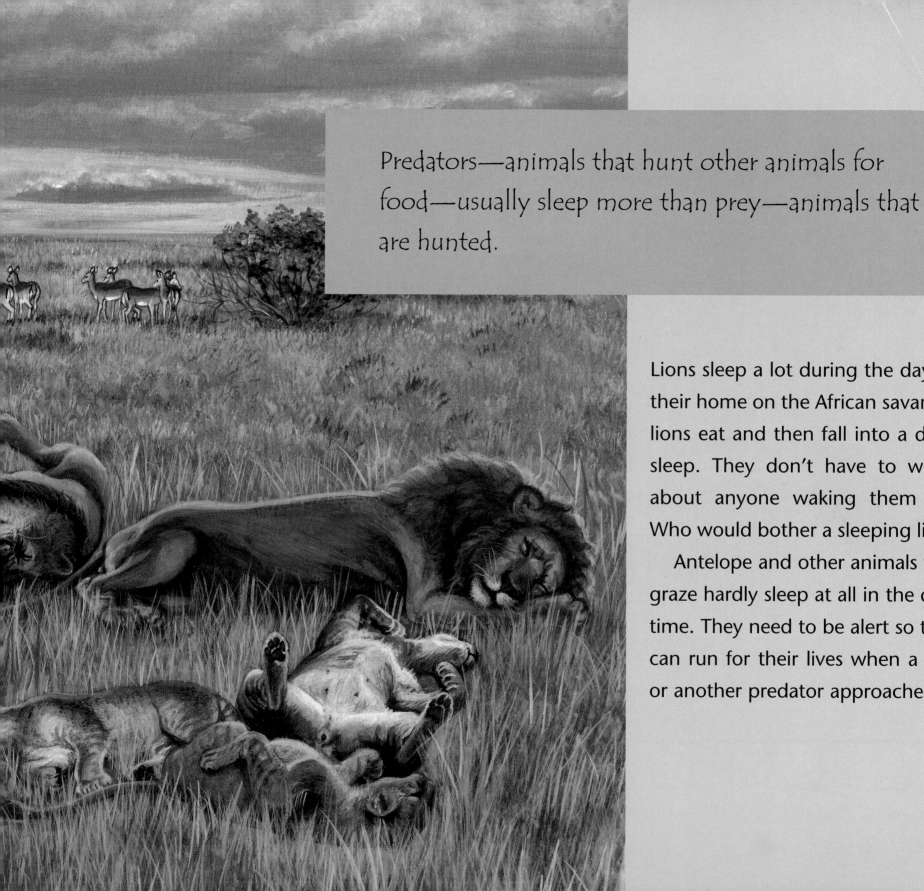

Predators—animals that hunt other animals for food—usually sleep more than prey—animals that are hunted.

Lions sleep a lot during the day. In their home on the African savanna, lions eat and then fall into a deep sleep. They don't have to worry about anyone waking them up. Who would bother a sleeping lion?

Antelope and other animals that graze hardly sleep at all in the daytime. They need to be alert so they can run for their lives when a lion or another predator approaches.

Animals sleep in all kinds of places.

The endangered mountain gorillas that live in Africa's Virunga Mountains sleep in nests of leaves and branches. Each gorilla makes a new nest in a different tree every night.

Only babies and young gorillas under three years old sleep with their mothers. The large male silverback leader of the troop builds his nest on the ground at the foot of the tree where he can protect his family.

Not all animals sleep lying in a bed
or curled up in a cozy nest.

Three-toed sloths that live in the tropical rainforests of Central and South America sleep hanging upside down in the trees. Their long, sharp-clawed toes curve backwards, just right for hooking over a branch.

At night, when they're asleep, their body temperature cools off until it is almost the same as the air around them. In the morning the sun warms them again.

Although horses can lie down, they usually sleep standing up with their legs locked so they don't fall. They sleep only about three hours a day, but not all at once. Over a 24-hour period, horses get drowsy and sleep a few minutes at a time.

Some animals sleep at night,
and some sleep during the day.

Animals that sleep at night and are active in the daytime are called *diurnal.* Most people are diurnal. Cheetahs, giraffes, and eagles are examples of diurnal animals.

Animals that sleep in the daytime and are active at night are called *nocturnal.* Cats, mice, and owls are examples of nocturnal animals.

Most anteaters are nocturnal. Early in the morning the giant anteater of South America wraps its long bushy tail around itself like a blanket. Then it sleeps all day. At night it looks for its favorite foods— ants, of course, and termites.

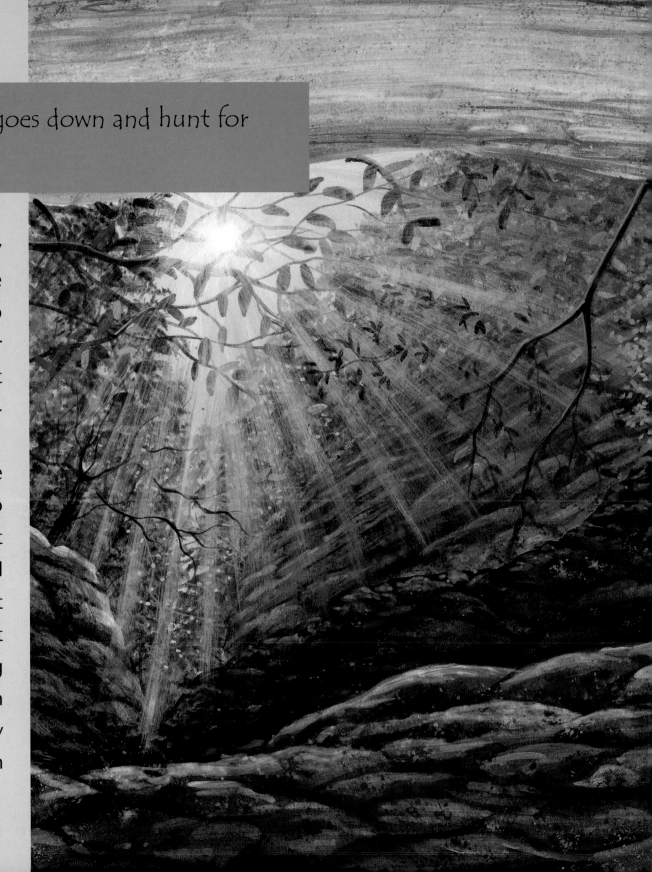

Bats wake up when the sun goes down and hunt for food after dark.

Some kinds of bats sleep all day hanging upside down from the roofs of caves. Other kinds sleep hanging from rafters in barns or from branches of trees. At night the bats fly out to look for something to eat.

Little brown bats, one of the most common bats native to North America, sometimes roost during the day in dark, humid places like caves. These bats hunt at night, feeding on insects that are also active during the evening hours. Little brown bats weigh less than half an ounce, but they can eat half their body weight in insects each night.

Many kinds of animals sleep soundly throughout the colder months of the year. This type of winter sleep is called hibernation.

Hibernating animals such as woodchucks and hedgehogs prepare for winter by eating a lot in the late summer and fall. By the beginning of winter, their bodies are fat and full of stored energy. A hibernating animal can survive without eating again until spring.

The ground squirrel eats until its weight almost doubles, then digs a burrow in the ground. When winter comes, it crawls in and curls up tightly. Its body temperature drops, almost to freezing, and its heart beats much more slowly. These changes enable the animal to go into a deep sleep for a long period of time. Every few weeks it wakes up and moves around the burrow, then goes back to sleep.

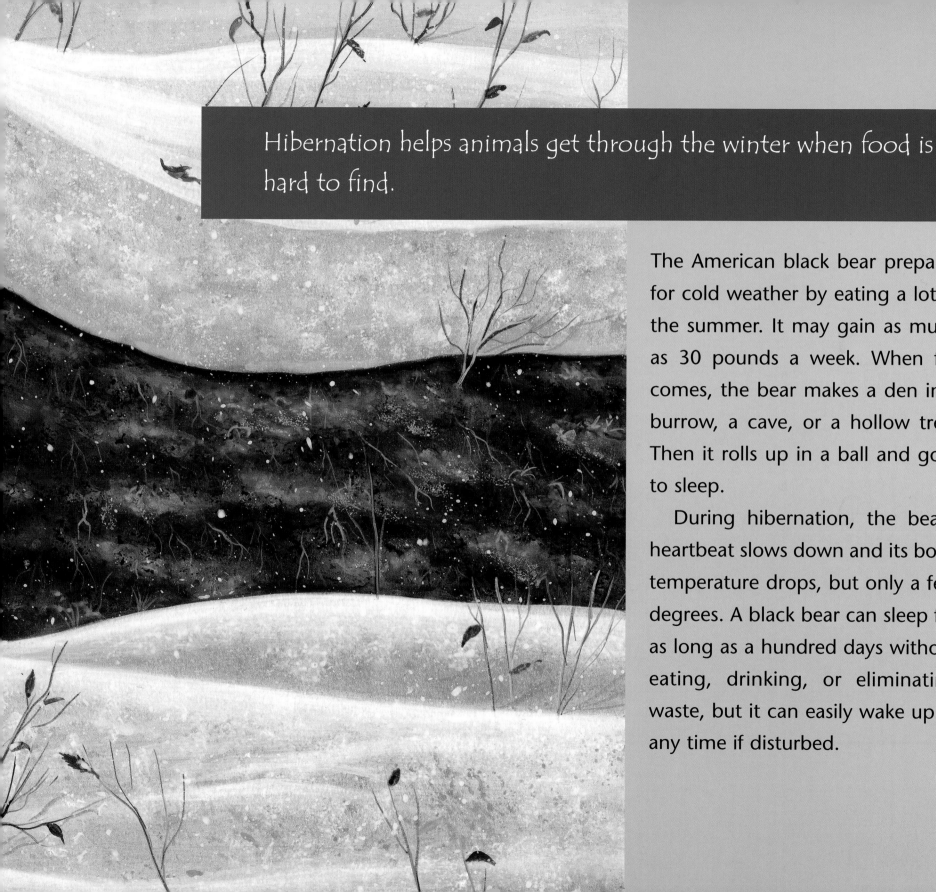

Hibernation helps animals get through the winter when food is hard to find.

The American black bear prepares for cold weather by eating a lot in the summer. It may gain as much as 30 pounds a week. When fall comes, the bear makes a den in a burrow, a cave, or a hollow tree. Then it rolls up in a ball and goes to sleep.

During hibernation, the bear's heartbeat slows down and its body temperature drops, but only a few degrees. A black bear can sleep for as long as a hundred days without eating, drinking, or eliminating waste, but it can easily wake up at any time if disturbed.

Insects don't sleep the way most animals do, but they can go into a resting state called *torpor*.

Torpor is not a deep sleep like hibernation, and it doesn't last as long. When an insect is in a state of torpor, its body slows down and stops growing.

The giant weta, a kind of cricket that lives in the mountains of New Zealand, can grow up to six inches long. It weighs twice as much as a mouse and is the heaviest insect in the world. The temperature sometimes drops below freezing in the mountains, but this doesn't bother the giant weta. During the night, the big insect freezes solid, like an ice cube. In the morning, it thaws out and crawls around just like a normal insect.

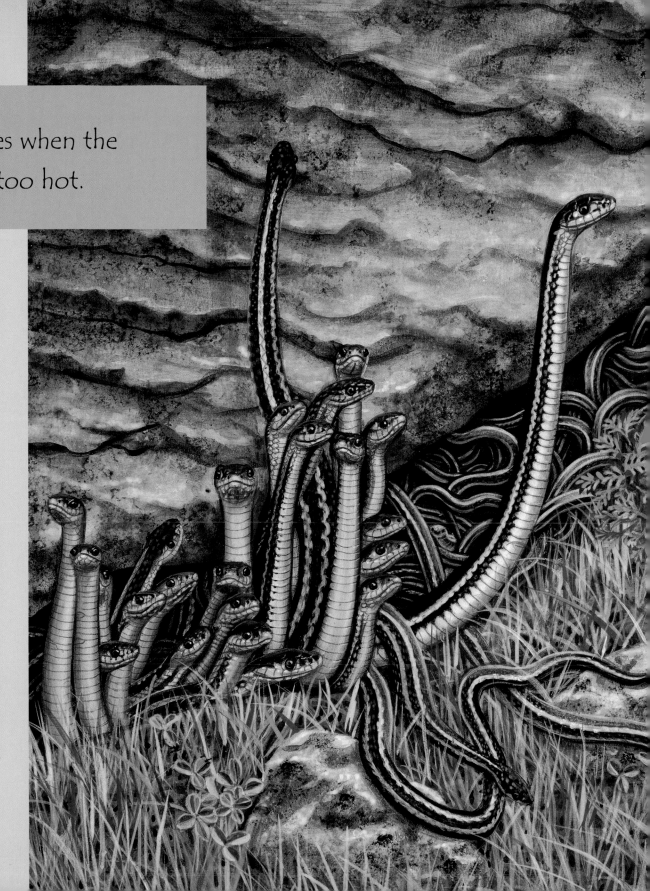

Snakes sleep in protected places when the temperature gets too cold or too hot.

In desert climates, snakes stay in the sun until the hottest part of the day, then find a sheltered spot to rest. In colder climates, timber rattlesnakes, black rat snakes, and garter snakes hibernate during winter.

In Manitoba, Canada, thousands of red-sided garter snakes hibernate every year for eight months in large dens six feet underground. The dens must be deep because the snakes would freeze to death if they were closer to the icy surface. They lie on top of each other—sometimes in piles two feet deep—to keep warm. In the spring these snakes crawl out of the dens and warm themselves in the sun.

Most birds sleep lightly, awakened easily by even a small sound.

Many birds sleep in a nest with their bills tucked under a wing. Some birds sleep while standing on one leg, perched on a branch, or floating on the water. Some can even sleep while flying.

Swifts spend most of their lives in the air. Some may spend two to three years flying before landing to breed in cliffs, in tall trees, or on buildings. When they sleep, they fly slowly at altitudes as high as 10,000 feet. Over their lifetime, some swifts fly 2.8 million miles, a distance equal to a hundred times around the Earth.

Mammals that live in the ocean take many short naps instead of sleeping soundly for long periods.

Ocean mammals like dolphins and whales need to come to the surface frequently to breathe. They sleep near the ocean's surface so they can easily and quickly come up for air.

Dolphins sleep while swimming. They take little naps by letting half of their brain sleep at a time. While one half of the brain sleeps, the other half is awake, alerting the animals to surface and breathe. Dolphins spend about eight hours a day napping on and off.

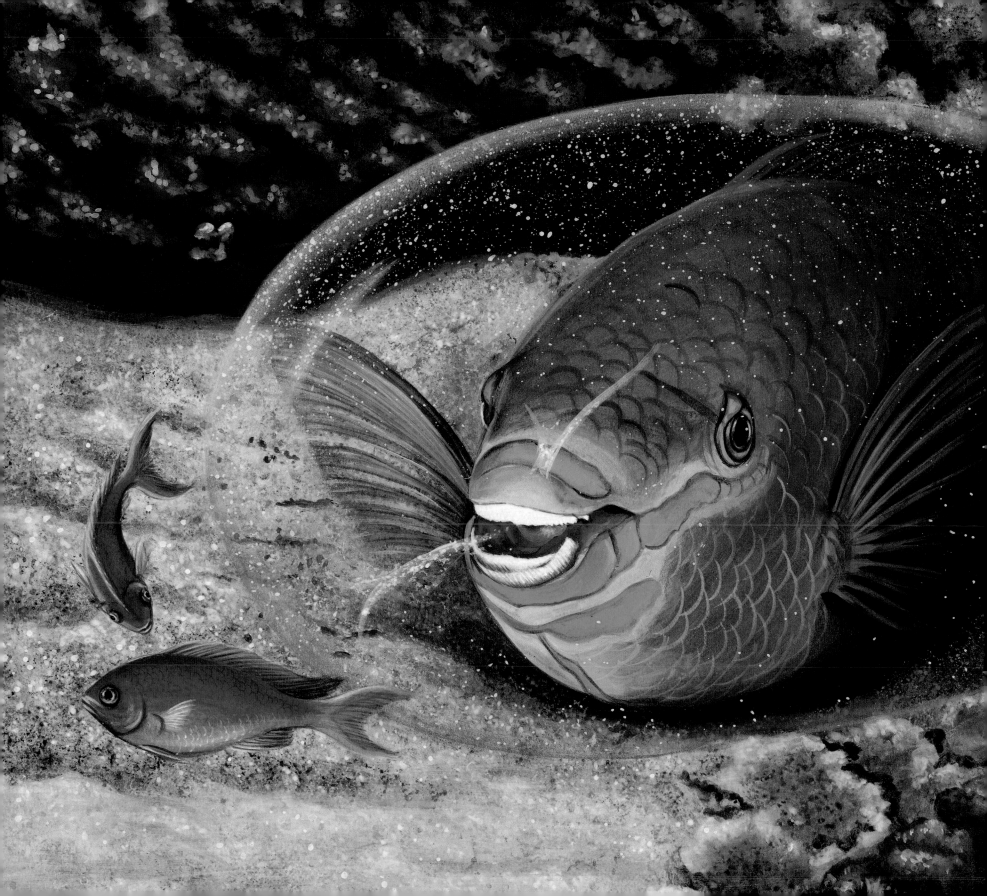

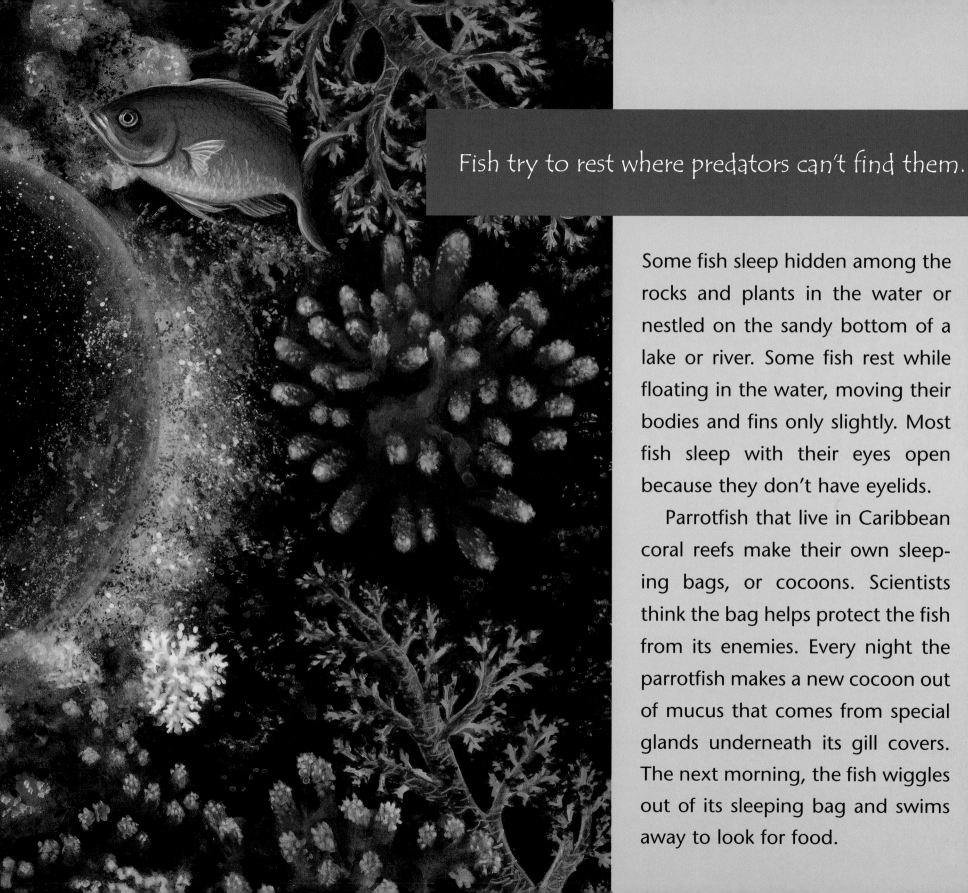

Fish try to rest where predators can't find them.

Some fish sleep hidden among the rocks and plants in the water or nestled on the sandy bottom of a lake or river. Some fish rest while floating in the water, moving their bodies and fins only slightly. Most fish sleep with their eyes open because they don't have eyelids.

Parrotfish that live in Caribbean coral reefs make their own sleeping bags, or cocoons. Scientists think the bag helps protect the fish from its enemies. Every night the parrotfish makes a new cocoon out of mucus that comes from special glands underneath its gill covers. The next morning, the fish wiggles out of its sleeping bag and swims away to look for food.

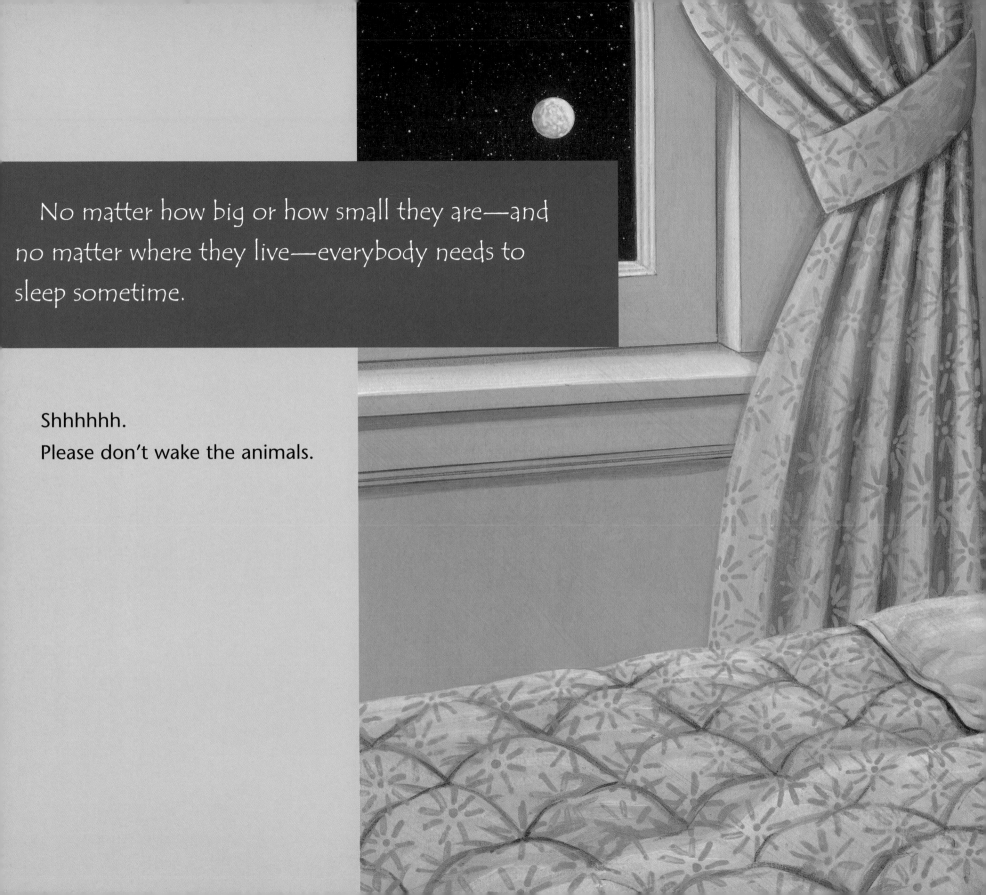

No matter how big or how small they are—and no matter where they live—everybody needs to sleep sometime.

Shhhhhh.
Please don't wake the animals.

The following books and websites will help you learn more about animal sleeping habits.

BOOKS

Animals Asleep by Robert Matero, 2000.

Animals at Rest by Susanne Riha, 1999.

Sleep and Rest in Animals by Corine Lacrampe, 2003.

WEBSITES

Center for Sleep Research

http://www.npi.ucla.edu/sleepresearch/encarta/Article.htm

Neuroscience for Kids, "How Much Do Animals Sleep?"

http://faculty.washington.edu/chudler/chasleep.html

San Diego Zoo, "Gorilla Facts"

http://www.sandiegozoo.org/animalbytes/t-gorilla.html

Sleep Habits

http://library.thinkquest.org/03oct/02063/animals-02.html